CHILDREN AT
WAR
WAR

Edited by Patricia Williams

PET

Published by BBC Educational Publishing
a division of
BBC Enterprises Limited
Woodlands
80 Wood Lane
London W12 0TT

First published 1989. Reprinted 1989, 1990, 1991
© Cable and Satellite Enterprises Limited 1989

Edited by **Lisa Hyde**
Cover and book design by **Keith Crawford**
Picture Research by **Joanne King**

ISBN 0 563 34406 7

Set in ITC Garamond Book
Typeset by Ace Filmsetting Ltd, Frome, Somerset
Text printed in Great Britain by Mackays of Chatham
Cover printed by Fletchers Ltd

Front Cover: *tl* Novosti Press Agency; *c* Hulton Picture Company; *r* IWM; *cl* Hulton Picture Company; *c* IWM; *r* Bettmann/Hulton Picture Company; *bl* IWM; *r* Novosti Press Agency
Back Cover: Hulton Picture Company

p4 Novosti Press Agency; pp6–7 Hulton Picture Company; p8*tl* Lewis Chester; *br* IWM; p9 Keystone Press Agency; p11 & p12*tl* Helmut Sontag; p12*br* IWM; p13*t* UPI; *b* IWM; p15*tl* & *br* Lehtikova; p16*t* Associated Press; *br* Riitta Karikoski-Chohda; p18 South African Library; p19 Denis Herbstein; p20*t* South African Library; *bl* Denis Herbstein; p22 The Polish Library; p23*l* Studium Polski Podziemnej; *r* Jan Ciechanowski; p24 Studium Polski Podziemnej; p26 Aéro-Photo; p27*tr* IWM; *b* Roger-Viollet; pp29–30 Isetta Malagoli; p32 Cork Examiner; p33*tr* Hugh Leonard; *br* National Library of Ireland; p35 Joanna Kloots; p36*t* & *b*, p37*tl* Rijksinstituut voor Oorlogsdocumentatie; p37*br* Joanna Kloots; p39*l* IWM; p39*r* & p40*l* Tenby Museum; p40*br* IWM; p41 Tenby Museum; pp43–44*l* Premila Deva; p44*br* India Office; p46 Akihiro Takahashi; p47*t* IWM; *b* Kyodo News Service; p48*l* John Launois/Curtis/Camera Press; *tr* Kyodo News Service; *br* Akihiro Takahashi

ABBREVIATIONS: IWM = Imperial War Museum; UPI = United Press International

CONTENTS

Chronology

1922 Musssolini takes power in Italy

1923 Hitler attempts and fails to seize control in Germany

1933 Hitler becomes Chancellor of Germany

1935 Italy invades Abyssinia (now Ethiopia)

1936 Germany re-occupies the Rhineland
Germany and Italy establish the Rome–Berlin 'axis'

1938 Germany and Austria united ('Anschluss')
Munich agreement

1939 March: Czechoslovakia annexed
August: Germany makes non-aggression pact with Russia
1 Sept: Germany invades Poland
3 Sept: WAR DECLARED on Germany by Britain and France
Russia invades Poland and Finland

1940 Germany invades Denmark, Norway, France, Low Countries
10 May: Churchill becomes British Prime Minister
May: Belgium and Holland surrender
May: Evacuation from Dunkirk
Italy declares war, France signs armistice
Sept: Battle of Britain
Sept: German 'Blitz' of British cities begins

1941 June: Germany invades Soviet Union
Dec: Japan attacks Pearl Harbor
Dec: USA joins the war

1942 Spring: Japanese advance through south Asia
Autumn: British and US advances in north Africa
Nov: Soviet Union counter-attacks Germany

1943 Jan: German surrender to Russians at Stalingrad
May: Axis surrender to Allies in Tunisia
Autumn: Italy changes sides

1944 June: Allied landings in Normandy
Sept: American troops in Germany

1945 April: Final offensive in Italy
25 Apr: US and Soviet troops meet on the Elbe
28 Apr: Mussolini killed
30 Apr: Hitler kills himself
1 May: Soviet Union controls Berlin
3 May: British recapture Rangoon in Burma
7 May: Formal SURRENDER of Germany
6 Aug: Atom bomb dropped on Hiroshima in Japan
9 Aug: Atom bomb dropped on Nagasaki in Japan
2 Sept: SURRENDER of Japan

The Banana War

By LEWIS CHESTER

Lewis Chester lived in the East End of London with his parents. Because of the docks, the armament factories and the vital oil tanks, this area became a prime target for German bombs. Children like Lewis were sent away to safer homes in the country leaving their family and everything they knew behind to embark on the adventure of evacuation.

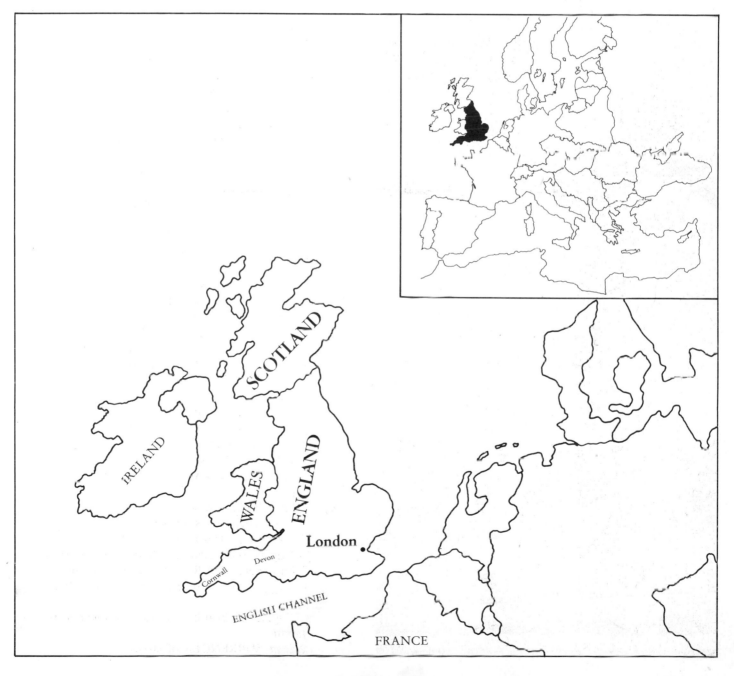

SCOTLAND

IRELAND

WALES

ENGLAND

London

Devon

Cornwall

ENGLISH CHANNEL

FRANCE

My experience of war was shaped by the banana. Whenever kids and adults would meet, at home, in the streets or in the snug of an air raid shelter, the older generation would sing the praises of this amazing fruit - only available in times of peace.

To me the banana became a symbol of all the joys to come, a fruit that would not only melt deliciously in your mouth but also dissolve all human pain and suffering. In those dark days, hopes of the banana kept my spirits up. Somehow the war managed to end and the sea lanes to the West Indies became safe again and I, aged nine, was presented with my longed-for first banana. I detested it.

Years later I had another go, but I was right the first time. The experience taught me a lot of things - don't believe everything those in charge tell you, there's no substitute for first-hand knowledge and don't build your hopes on fruit.

In London the war was bad for our schooling but good for our education. Had Hitler behaved himself, I don't think I would have moved very far from my home patch near Blackwall Tunnel in the East End. As it was I travelled to Cornwall and Devon and finally to Wales. So by the end of it I had the sense of living in a country rather than lurking in a few back streets.

There was a lot of sadness and homesickness about evacuations, but there was a lot of adventure too. It was the adults who had the really thin time of it. My father disappeared from my world at an early stage. He worked for the borough cleansing department on a job that meant he didn't have to go into the army. During the Blitz he used to drag bodies out of the rubble on the Isle of dogs. Unable to bear the work, he volunteered for the army, asking only that he be excused from the infantry. So they put him in the Durham Light Infantry.

He was one of the lucky ones. He survived, but I don't remember seeing him again until after the banana. I managed to cling on to my mother a little longer. Indeed, she tells me she was holding my hand in the Grand Cinema - 'watching another of your terrible Tom Mix cowboy films' - when the first

Children being evacuated during the Blitz on to waiting trains. Metropolitan Policewomen help to keep their spirits up.

6

Anxious watchers at the station barrier wait for their parents' arrival on the first 'evacuation special' from London.

bombing raid on the docks occurred. I don't remember that but I vividly remember the mass shelters of the period. We used to favour the crypt of All Saints' Church and the basement of the electricity showrooms in the East India Dock Road.

I liked the showroom best. It was warm, they had bunks for which there was a lot of friendly rivalry and they ran raffles. My first positive memory of childhood, aged four, is an exciting one – winning a large white canvas shopping bag in the basement raffle.

The bombs held no terrors for me. Quite the reverse, when they were actually falling I was usually experiencing an extra strong cuddle. But when the Blitz got too bad, my mother hauled me off to Cornwall. I remember learning the 'Three Rs' in a little school on a cliff. Down below there was this extraordinary thing called the sea. One morning I remember being awestruck by the sight of a dead whale on the beach. But I was so small, it could have been a dead haddock.

My mother joined the air force, so I went back to the East End where I was lodged with my grandparents. This was normal in the East End then – as it is in the West Indies today. Grandparents did most of the child-rearing while the parents were off working or whacking Hitler.

We lived in a tiny two up, two down on Dee Street. That is, we lived in the two up, the two down was occupied by a young widow (her husband's ship had been torpedoed in the Atlantic) and her three children. Behind us was Ettrick Street, a row of bombed out shells that provided a marvellous adventure playground for us kids. Forbidden territory of course, but that made it all the more delightful.

I had a good time then. The widow was loving but fierce. She would really lay into her kids to raise them decent and I began to see the advantages of being an only child. You didn't get whacked for the misbehaviour of a brother or sister.

Lewis Chester (right) in Wales, 1942.

My grandmother was an oddity, being both very religious and funny. The edge of her tongue was much feared, especially by my grandfather, a tobacco-chewing old seaman and docker. He was a quiet man but he could do wonderful things. He could spit further and more accurately than any man in the neighbourhood, and he could blow beautifully formed smoke rings.

I was unhappy when they dragged me from all this and, for my own safety, had me evacuated to Wales. They sent me to a little mining village at the top of the Rhondda Valley, and it was lovely there. The house I was in backed directly on to the hills. Real country. The Welsh were nice to me too, particularly after they discovered I could sing. What I missed was mates. Then a really hard lot said I could join them if I passed the test. The leader explained that I would have to stand against a garage door while he shot arrows all round me. I knew he must be kidding so I stood against the garage door and he shot arrows, real ones, all round me. But I was in the gang and able to take part in the great wave of South Wales orchard burglaries in 1944.

Wales was good to me. I flew my first kite there. I got to peer down a Welsh girl's knickers, though it was too dark to make anything out. I had my first unbroken year of schooling there which did me no great harm. Aside from the regular bed-wetting, the evacuees' most common complaint, I have only two unhappy memories.

I used to go around with the boy in the family I lived with and sing Welsh songs for the relatives. They would readily pay for the pain of it, sixpence to the Welsh boy and threepence to me. I used to think this terribly unjust, though in reality it was kind of them to give me anything at all. I've only recently figured out why this should be so upsetting (in fact while writing this article). The problem was that I really did feel warm and family with them, but the money idea just put me at my distance, told me I was the outsider.

One day a dark-haired woman came all the way up from London to see me, claiming to be my mother. I knew this could not be. It was a long time since I had seen my mother but I knew, for sure, that she had beautiful blonde hair. At that age I had somehow not cottoned on to hair dyeing. Anyway, it was a very awkward visit which hurt me a bit at the time, and still hurts my mother to this day. When the rocket attacks on the East End eased off I went home to Dee Street. It was still there, miraculously untouched, though the wasteland around it had expanded. The same kids, though a bit bigger, were still dive-bombing each other in the playground of my old school.

But there were differences. Sweets seemed in more liberal supply and there was talk – far too early as it turned out – of an end to rationing. Another tell-tale sign was the fact that the corrugated iron shelter at the bottom of our yard had been donated to the cats.

But the biggest giveaway was the state of my grandparents and the grown-ups in the street. They were all getting more cheerful at the same time. Somehow I knew that the dream of my banana would soon become a reality.

Londoners take shelter in the Underground during the Blitz, 1940.

Many families built their own Anderson Shelters in readiness for bombing raids. Here a toy dog, in regulation gas mask, stands guard over the entrance.

A Child Soldier

By HELMUT SONTAG

When Hitler came to power in Germany in 1933 he enrolled not only adults but also children to help 'get the country back on its feet again'. The Hitler Youth Movement was a children's army, complete with its own uniform and drilled in military style to become disciplined, unquestioning disciples of Hitler's basic beliefs. In the later years of the war so stretched were German military reserves that even children were conscripted into the forces. Many of them were killed in action. Helmut Sontag was one who survived.

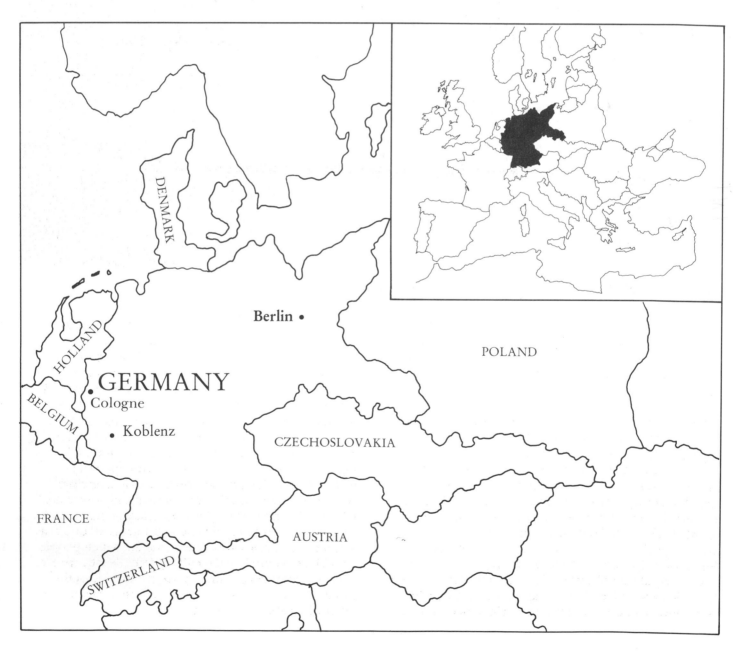

Seesport-Ausweis Nr. 11 / 0704

(Gebiets- / laufende)
Nummer

Dienst-
siegel

Sonny.

(Eigenhändige Unterschrift)

Sonntag Helmut

Name und Vorname

geb. am: 7.11.1929

Bann: 65   Gef.: 1

Die Richtigkeit
von Unterschrift und Bild bescheinigt:

Gebiets-Marine-Hitler-Jugend-Sachbearbeiter

Hitlerjungen mit bestandener B (K)- oder C (K)-
Prüfung gehören zur seemännischen Bevöl-
kerung und werden demnach für die Kriegs-
marine gemustert. Dieser Ausweis ist bei
der Musterung zum Wehrdienst vorzulegen.

Der Inhaber dieses Ausweises hat

vom _____ bis _____ 194

am **Seesportlehrgang AK** der

teilgenommen und die **AK-Prüfung**

mit _____ bestanden.

_____, den _____ 194

[Siegel]

Unterschrift des Prüfungsberechtigten

Helmut Sontag's Hitler Youth papers – complete with his name wrongly spelt!

I come from Wesseling, a district on the River Rhine between Cologne and Bonn, a town of some 7000 swelled in the later years of the war by 3000 foreign workers living in special camps.

My father was a veterinary surgeon who had served under Field Marshall Rommel in North Africa. So when I became a naval volunteer and my uniform was like my father's I felt very proud.

I was dying to go to war and not be a schoolboy any more and to get away from lessons, not that I was bad at them. I was first in German and first in history but I hated maths and music. My music teacher disliked me because he once heard me singing an English sea shanty (I didn't understand a word of it). 'How dare you do that,' he roared. 'A German boy from the Beethoven Gymnasium [School] singing enemy songs!'

One day at school I was told to go and report to the local Gestapo office. The Gestapo policed the civilian population and everyone was very frightened of them.

When I got to the office I gave a smart Hitler salute and a 'Heil Hitler!', although, in honesty, not many people where we lived went around saluting Hitler. They asked me a lot of difficult questions about my parents. Did they have contacts with foreigners? Did they listen to BBC broadcasts? I was angry at these insulting questions – didn't they know that my father was an army officer who had served under Rommel? Worse was to come. When I got home I found that my mother had been taken to the Gestapo Head-quarters near Cologne. My father was in a terrible state. We discovered that my mother had done a deal with one of the foreign workers, exchanging bread for soap which was unobtainable and a great luxury. This was technically black-marketeering for which people could be executed. It took all my father's influence, as well as a good deal of money, to get her released – which she was after three days. You can imagine our relief when she came home.

Helmut finally joins 'a real war'.

weather, after a beautiful autumn, was miserably cold and freezing. In the middle of all this I celebrated my sixteenth birthday.

Around this time I joined a special outfit called 'The Werewolves' which was being trained by the Waffen SS. We were supposed to sneak behind American lines. We wore American uniforms and learned to recognise the various American army ranks as well as the various kinds of American equipment. We were also told about these mysterious things called Hershey Chocolate Bars and Wrigley's Chewing Gum.

To do all this learning English was essential and we used to practise by listening to AFN – the American Forces Network on the radio. I remember how astonished we were when we heard American slang for the first time: there was a world of difference between that and our stiff 'school' English! But how we adored the AFN music which I heard even in my sleep. Listening to AFN certainly helped our English but I remember that one of the men, when practising American military commands, said 'OK' instead of 'Yes sir'. Our instructor had a fit.

Even an incident like this never made me think seriously about National Socialism. My parents were not Nazis but they were very wary of criticising either Hitler or the Nazi Party in front of us children. They were Catholics but avoided discussing the obvious conflict between Nazism and Catholic beliefs. My father once tried to give me a hint of this in a letter he wrote to me in 1940, but he never really spelled it out. My own view was simple: God was on one side and Hitler was on the other. There was no contact between them. If you started thinking about it too much, you might begin to ask what people were fighting for.

And anyway, I so wanted to be a soldier and leave school. I volunteered for the naval reserve in April 1944 and my call-up papers came at the beginning of July. I can remember my enormous excitement as I set off. I knew that this was the beginning of my own life – no more maths, no more music. This was a real war I was joining.

My uniform was a terrible fit. The belt was too wide, the trousers too long, the shirt too big, the boots too small and the socks too short. The jacket was so enormous that it hung down to my knees.

I only spent a short time in the naval reserve. By July 1944 there was not much left of the German Navy so I joined the Army in September 1944 which I didn't mind at all as many of my friends had also joined. My unit was sent to the Western Front near Aachen beyond the Rhine, not far from Wesseling. It was the Americans who were fighting in that sector rather than the British. The air raids were getting worse, especially around Cologne, and I began to wonder how much longer people could hold out. The

American soldiers arrive in Germany; the war is over.

We never got the chance to test our knowledge because just then the Americans broke through our lines around Julich and Linnich and there was heavy fighting. Many of my friends were killed or wounded. I myself was wounded and later received a medal.

I was captured on 9 March 1945 by American soldiers from the First Division. I had been part of a motorcycle unit stationed near a bridge which was attacked by American tanks. Many men from my unit were killed. I say 'men' but in fact the average age was only fifteen to eighteen years old. I was wounded when an American tank ran over my left leg. The doctor at the American military hospital spoke perfect German and I remember he said to me 'Hey young fella, what are you doing here?' The Americans were very nice. Because the hospital was so crowded I was moved to another hospital which was run by Catholic nuns. I was there for six weeks as my leg was so badly broken. When I was released the war was almost over.

I remember my time in the Army as one of the best of my life. It was a great adventure and very exciting. When you're young you don't think of the hardships. It was after the war that the worst hardships came.

Jewish refugees leave Germany, 1939.

German civilians flee Aachen after the city is battered by bombs after the Nazis refuse to surrender to the Allied forces.

Wartime Memories

By RIITTA KARIKOSKI-CHOHDA

Finland was and is strategically important in Northern Europe, sitting as it does on the Baltic Sea within a short distance of the Russian city of Leningrad. To ensure there was no trouble at its back door, the Russians invaded Finland within the first few months of war. To protect the children of Finland many were evacuated to neighbouring Sweden which remained neutral throughout the war. But with a grandmother in the north of Finland, neither Riitta nor her baby sister had to suffer the privations of evacuation abroad.

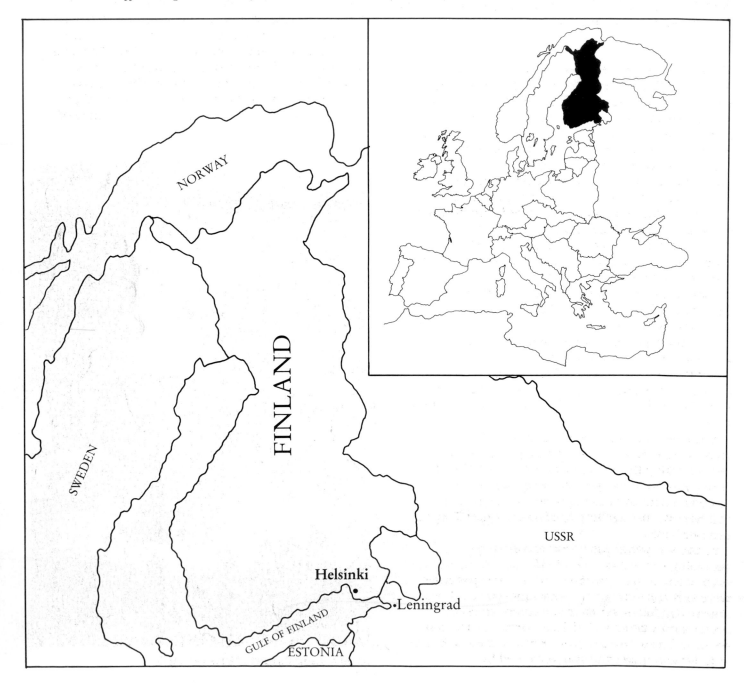

Dinnertime for girls involved in the war effort.

In Finland we had two wars. The first 'Winter War' with the Russians started on 30 November 1939. That same day I was to experience a feeling of fear repeated many times during the ensuing years.

In Helsinki 30 November was a clear, crisp winter's day. Suddenly an air raid siren sounded, my mother looked out pointing at seven aeroplanes in the sky. The following whistling sound and the crash were to become familiar noises. 'The Russians are here. The war has started', my mother explained, bundling my sister, the maid and me into the cellar of our block of flats. We came to know that place intimately. The image of those aeroplanes still haunts me. For years I had nightmares of the air raids.

Shortly afterwards my father left to serve in the General Headquarters. He had been a colonel in the Air Force. He was now recalled, later to become the head of the Operations Department. We were not to see much of him for five years.

For the remaining war period we lived in a society solely of women and children. I was seven and had started school the previous September. My sister was three.

With the increase of bomb attacks on Helsinki we were twice evacuated, the first time in 1940, the second during the 'Continuation War' in 1943. My sister and I were lucky not to have been sent to Sweden on our own, as happened to countless other children. We had the luxury of having a grandmother in a safe haven.

As the war progressed, food and clothing were becoming very scarce. Soon in Helsinki there weren't even potatoes, only hateful swedes. Other pet hates were herrings which were sometimes served three times a day; luncheon meat and cream crackers posted by my father's kind friends in Denmark; and rye crisp bread. Dried carrots replaced sweets. While in Helsinki our diet was supplemented by grandmother's parcels. The contents were always marked 'Books'. Trading in food and clothing outside the allowances was illegal, but the black market was strong and obvious. One hot summer's day I was fetching a parcel from the Post Office. The butter inside was melting and had left large grease marks on the wrapping. The clerk handing the parcel to me remarked: 'This is a very greasy book.'

I remember being perpetually hungry, more so towards the end of the war. I was growing faster then. The sense of hunger remained with me until the late 1940s. The lack of sweets also posed problems for us. In the schoolyard tar was being melted for laying the tarmac. When the workers weren't looking we would steal the tar for 'chewing gum'. We also chewed tree resin. War brought endless discomfort. Immediately after joining grandmother's school I contracted head lice and gave them to everybody around me. There was no medication to remove them. A head lice hunt ritual was established, mother having to pick them out one by one with a special comb. The hair was then washed with home-made soap made of boiled animal intestines. I can still remember the stench of that vile soap.

Bomb damage, Helsinki, November 1939.

Finnish ski troops bring in Russian prisoners after wiping out Russia's 44th Division during the Winter War.

With the continuation of the war things became better organised. In the absence of men the women did everything, drove trains, buses, streetcars and lorries, operated cranes, acted as mechanics. My sister and I collected cones for firewood, wild berries and mushrooms for food factories. I assisted in haymaking and tended to the horses on the farms. In cities, public parks were taken over for growing vegetables.

People became ingenious. What there was not was replaced by what there was: dandelion roots for coffee, raspberry leaves for tea, wood for shoes. But the health of children did not benefit from the wartime diet. White spots appeared on my nails, and on my neck I developed an Africa-shaped brown patch. The cause was lack of vitamins.

In the summer of 1944 we were, for the first time, to encounter other evacuees whose situation was far worse than ours – refugees from territories reinvaded by Russia. In the big farm in south-eastern Finland, where we were staying during the school holidays, families arrived with hardly anything but the clothes they were wearing. They were scattered in various houses belonging to the farm and settled down to work, later to be dispersed all over Finland. We played with the children picking up words of their dialect.

Finland was never occupied. To reclaim lost territories we co-operated voluntarily with the Germans. In Helsinki you realised there were foreign soldiers in your country, although you did not see much of them. You heard of the woman living in the flat above entertaining German friends, and the maid had boyfriends called 'Franz' and 'Fritz'. Some Russian officers came in after the war as part of the Soviet British Control Commission. They, however, had no contact with anybody. No 'Igors' or 'Ivans' became known to the maid. We had never seen Russians before. We looked with great curiosity at this foreign species with whom we had been fighting for so long.

Riitta and baby Eva in happier times, 1939.

16

White Sands and Stuffed Lions

By DENIS HERBSTEIN

Denis Herbstein was three when, 6000 miles away, Europe went to war. He lived in Muizenberg, a seaside resort on the suburban railway line between the city of Cape Town and the British Royal Navy port of Simonstown. With the Suez Canal closed, ships sailing from Britain to India, the Far East and Australia had to sail round the Cape.

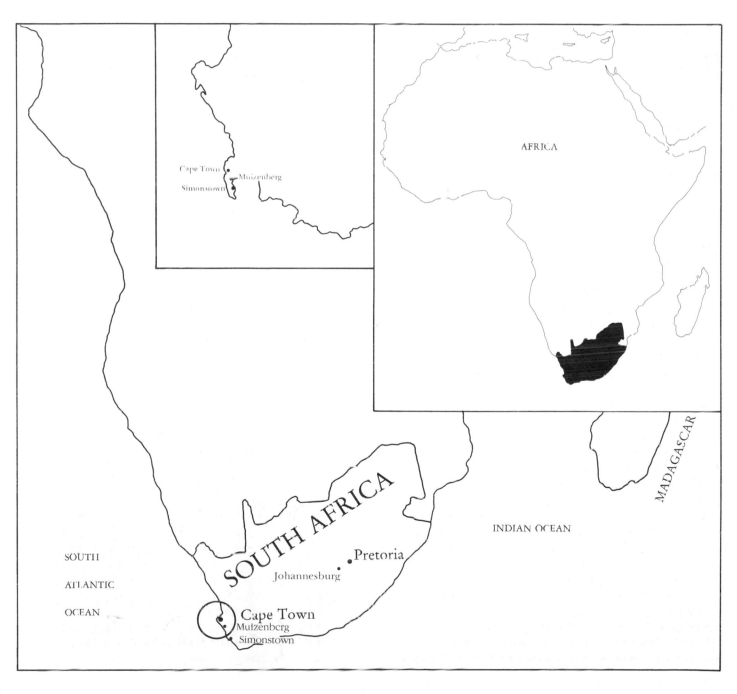

One day, soon after the war began, my father took a loving look at his new Pontiac car – the one with the running boards you see in old Hollywood gangster movies – and locked it in the garage. Petrol was scarce, so from now on he would have to travel the fifteen miles to his office by train.

My father, a solicitor in Cape Town, didn't join up and go 'up north' like some of my younger uncles and cousins. But he was a member of the home guard. One night there was a rumour that the Japanese were planning a landing. Dad's army was marched to the top of the mountain, and then halfway down again, and finding it was a false alarm they emptied their brandy flasks and returned home 'exhausted'. When we went for walks I had to keep in time to his 'Left, right, left, right, I had a dog and it left, it served me jolly well right, left right left, right . . .'

The real enemy were the Japanese. Despite all sorts of wild rumours nobody ever saw them, but they were there all right, their submarines lurking under the waves, perhaps an aircraft carrier drawing near under cover of the stormy Cape winter to drop bombs on courting couples on the promenade. Signs warned: 'DON'T TALK ABOUT SHIPS OR SHIPPING.' Our windows were blacked out at night, so that a potential invader would not be tempted to look through the window and see a game of bridge in progress. To this day my mother has the same royal-blue velvet 'black-out' curtains hanging in the lounge – but now they are closed in the daytime to keep the sun off her carpet.

In that lounge I had my earliest realisation that not everything was right with the world. My father, not one to show his feelings, was sitting in his armchair listening to a voice that crackled out of the wireless. Tears streamed off his cheeks, and he didn't seem ashamed. 'Churchill is speaking,' he said, 'remember this day.' Here was a man whose parents came from the heartland of eastern Europe, with only a mother-in-law from Middlesbrough to connect him to Britain's seemingly hopeless cause.

My grandparents lived round the corner. Did they have chickens? My mother thinks not, but I seem to remember fresh eggs in the basket I was forever lugging back and forth between mother and daughter. It was from Granny Becky's house, on the road running to the booms over the railway line, that my uncle Archie, freshly graduated from medical school, lifted me high in the air and went off to war. He is buried in a cemetery in the Egyptian desert, his grave fringed by bougainvillaea and frangipani flowers.

The suburban railway line continued south, to the terminus and Simonstown. Its most unusual commuter was Nuisance, a giant Great Dane who certainly knew what to do with drunken sailors. He would wait for them on the platform at Cape Town station and guide, nudge, maybe dog-handle them –

depending on how much they had imbibed – on to the midnight train. On arrival at Simonstown, he helped them off, barking urgently if they refused to wake up. He was a caring military policeman, and no conductor ever asked him for his ticket. The Royal Navy valued his services so highly he was made an honorary able seaman. On the one occasion I met up with 'AB' Nuisance, his head towered above mine. He left me alone. I had drunk nothing stronger than David and Salkow's Sparkling Orange.

'AB' Nuisance, our most unusual commuter.

Despite the war, Muizenberg's hotels were full in the Christmas holidays. To the white sands and multi-coloured bathing boxes and blue sea was added a new colour, khaki. The British servicemen wore funny, baggy shorts and had their pictures taken in the photographic parlour with the stuffed lions near the swing beach. The village was also the home of the Park Hotel, a convalescent hospital for sailors wounded at sea. My mother's war service was to get cakes from the wives of suburban Cape Town, thereby ensuring that the war-wounded enjoyed a tea to remind them of happier times.

Denis (left) with family on holiday at Slippery Rock in the Eastern Cape.

Muizenberg's Park Hotel, where sailors convalesced after being wounded at sea.

One night my parents were strolling down the promenade when they saw the police trying to persuade a rowdy drunk to descend from a lamp post. He was none other than the mild Aussie who had come to dinner the night before – and had been through hell in the fighting. There was a British sailor whom we saw for several months of nursing after being blown through two decks by a torpedo. He recovered, boarded another ship, still bound for India. It was torpedoed a few hours outside Simonstown. He didn't make it back to the Park Hotel.

Some white South Africans were on Hitler's side, admiring his racist, anti-Jewish sentiments. They blew up synagogues and painted nasty slogans, but we did not feel unduly threatened, though Muizenberg had a very large Jewish community fortunate to have left Germany and Poland a generation before. The one ugly note came from the Welthagen family, who lived in the first house as you drove in from town. A swastika, the flag of Nazi Germany, fluttered from their window, until they were threatened with prosecution. Black people, then as now the majority of the population, had no say on the decision to go to the war, but thousands volunteered and many are buried in Commonwealth War Graves up north.

Food was rationed, but the hardships were few. An aunt, the village grocer, organised food parcels for relatives in England and the soldiers in Abyssinia, then Egypt and finally Italy. We made ice cream in a bucket crammed with ice cubes, taking it in turns to crank the handle. My birthday party, on 21 December (the longest day of the southern year), was a male institution, with the boys playing cricket in the road, while the one girl guest, a daughter of an old friend of my parents from Johannesburg who had to be invited, watched bored from the *stoep* (veranda) until Mum called us in for the scoff.

Towards the end of the war I came back to school one afternoon having heard the lunchtime news, and so could proudly tell the big boys that President Roosevelt had died. Was it about then that Andy Andrews, the ill-tempered headmaster of Muizenberg School, called me into his study following a now-forgotten wisecrack and gave me two of the best, sending me racing up the stairs biting back my tears to rub my bottom on the stone steps whence I watched the navy target-shelling across the bay?

After the war, the Park Hotel was demolished and a school built on the site. Nuisance became a father but his offspring were unable to adjust to peacetime conditions. Petrol became easier to get. But when Dad opened up the garage, he found that the sea air had corroded the Pontiac's gleaming bodywork.

Meanwhile, I heard for the first time that had I lived on the continent of Europe the gas chamber would have got me.

Uncle Archie (right), who did not return from the war.

The Young Resisters

By JAN CIECHANOWSKI

In September 1939 Germany invaded Poland. At the hands of the Germans six million Polish citizens were either shot or died in concentration camps. Singled out for particularly cruel treatment was the Jewish population – half of those killed in Poland were Jews. A brave Resistance Movement grew up in Poland to fight the German invaders. Children as young as eight and nine became members of the Resistance. Every Pole who survived the war has a horror story to tell. This is the story of just one young boy.

I was nine in 1939 and I felt war's first effect on my life in the spring, a few months before the war actually began, when my father, an army officer, began to have less and less time for my little brother and me because of the increasing pressure of army affairs. The second effect was more welcome: release from the threat of private German and violin lessons planned to begin on 1 September. I had met both language-tutor and instrument and had little affection for either of them.

The third effect was our sudden and complete uprooting from our pre-war life in Grudziadz, near the German frontier. When my father went to the war front my mother, brother, our dog and I left for Warsaw and my mother's family.

Our station platform goodbyes were to be the last we would see of our father. He was wounded on the first day of the war, captured by the Germans and sent in a hospital train to the east of Poland. We never discovered what happened to him after that.

Yet he must have sensed what might be coming. When my mother wanted to pack another uniform with *our* things for him to wear when on leave with us in Warsaw, he told her not to bother, in an unusual voice which has always haunted me.

Before returning to Warsaw, we decided to spend some weeks in search of my father's regimental depot. But those nights of travelling, spent crouching in a trench beside our trembling dog while our train was being bombed, seeing bombed dead bodies sprawled out like great dolls, and making a frightening and forbidden journey through enemy lines, taught me early on that war meant something more terrible than surprise journeys and a sudden escape from unwanted school tutors.

In Warsaw we stayed at the house of my uncle, then a famous lawyer. He was taken hostage by the Germans along with other leading citizens as part of a German campaign to terrorise the Polish population into obedience. He was later released.

One day he came home looking very grim and slowly unscrewed the brass lawyer's plaque from his front door. The Germans had forbidden him to work because he refused to obey their order to dismiss all the Jewish barristers. A few days later he had his first heart attack. Soon afterwards a second killed him. It was only after his death that I was told he had been a founder-organiser of the Resistance Movement. No wonder there had always been a certain tense feeling in the house that he might be re-arrested.

In time my mother found a flat and my brother and I started a new school. In the summer of 1942, when I was twelve, I stayed at an uncle's house in Otwock, a pretty, sleepy little tourist resort near Warsaw. Standing on my uncle's balcony one sunny morning, I witnessed the worst thing I ever saw in my whole life. German police arrived and surrounded the Otwock

Polish Jews being rounded up in the Warsaw Ghetto.

Ghetto, a wired-off part of the town into which they had squashed all the Jews. They began marching off to the station columns of Jews carrying little bundles, the parents holding their children's hands. I then saw a smaller column of old people and toddlers being led in the opposite direction, towards a clearing in a wood. A lot of shots rang out from there. Two more little crocodiles of youngest and oldest were each followed by a volley of shots. I realised that all the old people and toddlers were being killed. Afterwards, some lorryloads of German police drove out of the clearing and stopped quite near me. They were joking and drinking cool, fizzy drinks from bottles quenching their thirst under the hot, burning sun. Some wore oilskin butchers' aprons. Most looked between thirty and forty and I thought they might well be fathers themselves. I don't have words for what I felt. I wanted to be sick. I gazed at them in horror, unable to understand why.

Soon after I became a Boy Scout. In Poland during the war, the secret Boy Scout movement was part of the Junior Resistance movement of freedom fighters. We were involved in minor sabotage against the Germans, painting anti-Nazi graffiti on walls, carrying messages to Resistance fighters, delivering underground newspapers, collecting German police car numbers. To equip us for future Resistance work we received lessons in first aid, map reading and deciphering Morse Code. Older Scouts received military training and some were involved in armed resistance.

In 1943, impatient for serious Resistance work, I persuaded a schoolfriend's father to take me into his Resistance unit. As a courier I was a sort of secret delivery-boy, sometimes of messages, sometimes of weapons. Two arms deliveries I especially remember. Once, with a small gun in my pocket, I realised too late that ahead were two German guards stopping and searching people. Luckily for me they picked on the young girl just in front of me so I passed unchallenged. Had they caught me I would have been shot.

Another day, sweltering in a heavy overcoat in hot sun to hide a sten gun, I sweated still more when a German jeep slowly approached. Though longing to run, I forced myself to stroll, slowly and relaxed, and the jeep finally passed by. The fear that I felt at these moments lives with me even today.

The young girls involved in Resistance work 'laughed a lot and never showed fear'.

Our beloved Irish setter died resisting the Germans. They tried to steal him as they did many handsome dogs, but he refused to go. So they shot him and left him lying in the road. He had originally been brought from Scotland by my father's friend but, loving my father more than his owner, had kept running away to our house. So finally the friend gave him to us. At one point in our early wartime wanderings around Poland the dog had suddenly begun to whimper excitedly during a train-halt in the sidings. Later we found out that my wounded father's hospital train had also halted there for a while around that time.

I was fourteen when the Warsaw Uprising started. I began it as a messenger but within two weeks was a rifle-carrying soldier, the youngest of the unit's many young boys. The Girl Guides, again secretly involved in Resistance activities, tended our wounded. Many were only fourteen but their courage was incredible. They braved heavy gunfire to collect the wounded, deliver food, medicine and messages. Yet they laughed a lot and never showed fear. Our chief dread was of being wounded, because the hospital conditions were so bad. I saw children, some even as young as nine, acting as messengers, and Boy Scouts delivering mail, acting as couriers and repairing telephone lines. During the Uprising I bumped into a cool-headed Englishman I already knew well, through my family. He was an escaped prisoner of war who had managed to get from Germany to Warsaw. He was sending wireless reports to London. In fact, he acted as the special correspondent on the Warsaw Uprising to *The Times* newspaper!

These are the three most disturbing moments of the Uprising for me. The first was the death of the boy beside me who had just come to check that I was all right. The second was the pain and sadness of a pretty girl when she realised she was badly wounded in the face (she later needed a lot of plastic surgery). The third was the moment when I felt sure that the next bomb to hit the building we were fighting from would kill me. Imagine the relief I felt when at that moment the German planes flew off.

Jan and his father in 1934, in the park near the barracks where his father was a Colonel in command of a regiment.

We began the Uprising full of youthful spirits, thinking other countries would come to our aid. But by its end we were hungry, dirty, weary, defeated and without hope of help. I was terribly sorry for the civilians of Warsaw who had spent this awful time in cellars without proper food, light or anything to do but pray and wait. The children became pale and thin. Unable to feed her dog, a lady begged me to shoot him, but I just couldn't. When people finally left the cellars they found themselves surrounded by the ruins of what was once Warsaw.

After the Uprising I was taken prisoner and spent the last months of the war in Germany. When peace was declared in May 1945 I was only fifteen. In those six years of war I had lived a lifetime and my childhood now seemed so very far away.

During the Warsaw Uprising these young boys, like Jan, acted as secret messengers for the Resistance Movement.

Curfews and Resistance

By MARIE-CHRISTINE GOUIN

France was invaded by Germany on 8 May 1940, months after war began. Shortly afterwards France surrendered, signing a peace treaty with Germany in June. As in all countries occupied by the Nazis the Jewish community was singled out, and many of them were imprisoned in concentration camps like Auschwitz. Most of them never survived. Marie-Christine's mother was Jewish. For her those war years were spent in a state of fear dodging capture. Many of her family were not so lucky.

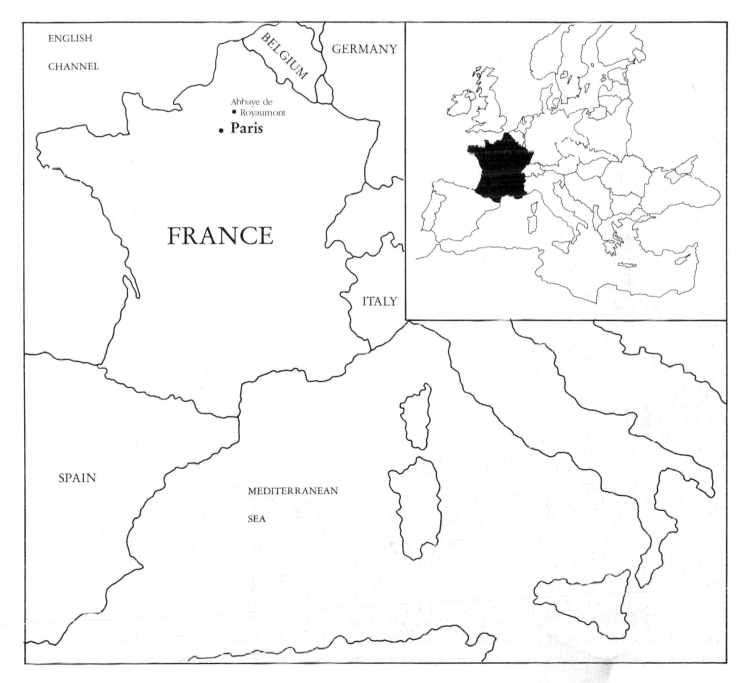

I was eight when war broke out, my sister was eighteen months younger. We lived in Paris but my parents also had a country house, the Abbaye de Royaumont, an old abbey 35 kilometres from Paris. Before the war the Abbaye was a cultural centre. For one year during the war it became a hospital. I remember seeing a wounded man with a bandage around his head and this gave me nightmares for weeks afterwards.

My mother was Jewish and had to wear a yellow star. My sister and I were classed as Aryans by the Germans so we didn't have to. Thank goodness my sister and I did not have to wear that yellow star. Our friends who did were horribly taunted. My mother like all Jews had to submit to humiliating restrictions which she bore with great dignity. Not only was she forbidden to leave Paris, she wasn't even allowed to go out after 8 o'clock at night. Despite all this my mother tried to make our lives as normal as possible. It was only after the war that I realised how much she must have suffered and how much her health had been harmed by all the stress she had endured.

Many of her friends and relations were sent to the concentration camps and she lived in dread of a knock at the door. But she had a friend in the police who would often warn her not to enter certain Metro stations on a particular day as the Germans planned to search them for Jews to send away.

It was such a miracle that my mother survived, particularly since our street was full of Gestapo offices! The Gestapo had taken over many of the empty houses for themselves and my mother used to wake up in the morning and hear the marching feet, wondering if they would stop outside her house. They never did.

My father was in the French Army in 1940 and was a prisoner of war after the fall of France. He was sent to a camp in Germany where conditions were not too bad. My mother sent him parcels and he was able to write to us regularly. My father was a good pianist and used to play in some of the camp concerts. These were such difficult years for my mother, living with two small children in that big house. My father was released in 1943 just after my mother discovered that her brother, a fine concert pianist, had been arrested in Grenoble. He died in Auschwitz.

Shortly after my father returned from Germany, he paid a visit to some Jewish friends and when he got there he found the family being taken away by the Germans. One of the children was my own age and he never came back.

It still puzzles me that my parents never realised what danger my mother was in. My cousin's husband had made sure that she got away to America and several other relations also went to America. I can only say that so many Jewish people at that time

The Abbaye de Royaumont, where Marie-Christine sheltered during the war years. It was also converted into a hospital.

simply never realised what was happening in the concentration camps, not until it was far too late. We only realised the full horror after the Liberation. It was only then that my mother found out what had happened to her brother.

Towards the end of 1943 the air raids in Paris got worse and my parents decided to send my sister and me to Royaumont where we stayed until the end of the war. Mother was smuggled out to join us.

As the Allies came nearer to Paris, we could hear clearly the sounds of the bombardment. We would climb up the tower to try and see it as well. The tower was used as a marker by pilots and several planes crashed near us. The local people would help the pilots who had to bale out, but such was the secrecy surrounding these activities that we never discovered until after the war that the man who ran the farm at Royaumont was a prominent member of the Resistance. We often listened to the BBC and I was fascinated by the *messages personnels*, coded messages for the Resistance.

When the Germans retreated from Paris, some units spent two nights at Royaumont, much to our alarm as my mother was hiding there at the time. I remember that my sister and I were in the middle of rehearsing a play but we were determined that we would not put it on as long as the Germans were there. Actually, they were quite decent. They were also a sad sight, many of them could not have been more than fifteen or sixteen. After they left, the officer in charge wrote my mother a nice letter thanking her for all her help!

When the Liberation came, it was the Americans who arrived first. We were so excited, jumping up and down and waving our flags. The soldiers threw us bars of chocolate but warned us that there still might be Germans around. After the Liberation parcels full of wonderful things began to arrive from our relatives in America. We returned to Paris in October 1944 and went back to school.

My father, in what was thought to be a very strange action, made us learn German. He thought it was a lovely language but this was not an opinion shared by many people in France at the end of the war.

A French woman rejoices during the Liberation.

French Jews at a concentration camp at Drancy. Marie-Christine's mother was Jewish and this could have been her fate.

Otto and Clocher

By ISETTA MALAGOLI

Italy had been ruled by the fascist dictator Mussolini since 1922. By 1936 Germany and Italy were political partners. Isetta Malagoli's father served in the North African campaign during the war, and the peace of 1943 was an emotional moment for all the family.

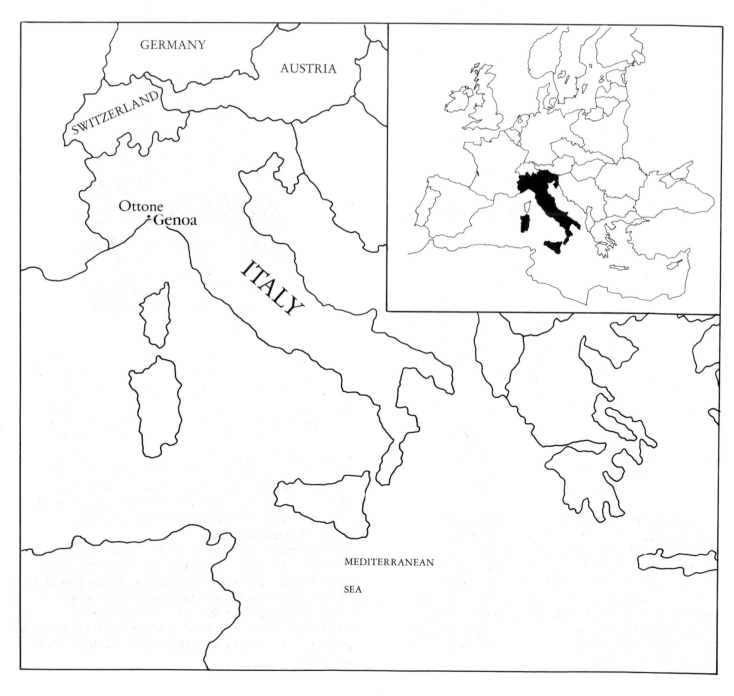

My parents and older brother Tato lived with my great-grandmother on the top floor of a tall medieval watchtower overlooking the beautiful countryside around our village, Ottone, some 80 kilometres from Genoa. One day a young boy rushed up the stairs to our flat with the news that a column of German soldiers was on its way to our village. The flags were swiftly taken in for fear of German anger at our celebrations, and the soldiers passed without stopping. From that moment until the winter of 1944 there was a constant flow of defeated German troops making their way back to their homeland.

We all knew there was a war on and we knew from overheard grown-up talk that there were the Germans, the Fascists, the partisans, the *Carabinieri* (police), and the 'Mongolians' – the Russian prisoners who had joined the German army. But in our small village there were only a few partisans, a handful of *Carabinieri*, our families, the sun, the river and our games, where we belonged to different gangs. These competed to obtain the most secret information: where the girls were hidden to be kept out of the way of the Germans; who among the locals was a partisan; where two English airmen were hidden after landing by parachute on a nearby hill; where the families had hidden their radios, binoculars and cameras. We had great mock battles, but we all wanted to be famous local partisan leaders rather than play the part of the Germans, because then we would have to lose and be shot.

Our most important activity, however, was to search for weapons thrown away by the Germans on their way home. We found a great many: pistols, bullets and the belts to put them in. But the most prized find was the rifle. It would never have been discovered if I, the youngest, hadn't let the side down. From that moment our weapons were taken away, including our beautiful German pistols which we had painted in various garish colours in order to disguise them. Also stopped was a wonderful game we had invented where we mixed the gunpowder from the bullets with potassium tablets and sulphur powder, and placed it between two large stones in one of the abandoned houses of the district. We then dropped a large stone on to the mixture from a good height and the gunpowder would then explode with a great bang.

But one effect of war that wasn't so pleasant was the lack of food. So Christmas, usually a time for feasting, was bleak for many. My parents fortunately had thought ahead and in March had bought two turkey chicks. Christmas morning arrived, the church bells were ringing and our father had already lit the fires. We went into the living room in our pyjamas and under the tree there were nuts, tangerines and a few toys. My father spent all morning attending to the turkeys in the kitchen.

By two o'clock everything was ready. My great-grandmother, dressed in black and wearing a choker with a gold brooch, was already sitting at the head of the table. My brother and I, with well-combed hair and brightly shining shoes, anxiously awaited our father so that we could sit down. Enrichetta, our maid, was in the kitchen ready to serve at table. Totally unexpectedly we heard footsteps outside the door. Then we heard a few loud knocks. The door opened and our maid called my father in a strained voice. Three German officers and a soldier appeared at the door of our living room. They clicked their heels and bowed to my great-grandmother. She remained still and regal at the head of the table. My mother took us by the hand and said: 'Come with me and I will give you a delicious roll with cheese.' For us the war had arrived.

The medieval watchtower at Ottone.

In the kitchen we found even more Germans. Other places were laid at our table. We did not know where to put ourselves, we felt strangers in our own home and huddled near the window. Enrichetta prepared a tureen of soup and asked me and my brother to spit in the tureen but not to tell my mother. We enjoyed our revenge. But then the turkey was taken into the living room. Enrichetta had just enough time to make us lick it – it was magnificent and had a wonderful taste. In all the rest of my life I have never eaten, seen or smelt a turkey like that stolen from me that wartime Christmas Day.

The Germans were to stay in our flat for a long time because its position was of strategic importance as it overlooked all the local roads. During the daytime the soldiers would roam the countryside on mules seeking out partisans while we played with our gunpowder mixture. In the evening we all returned to our home –the Germans, ourselves, the 'Mongols' and the mules.

Two Germans called Otto and Clocher had taken over our room and two had occupied our great-grandmother's room. We two children slept with our father and mother in their very large bed. Sometimes Otto took me in his arms and showed me photographs of his four-year-old daughter whom he had never seen.

The life led by the Germans in our home sometimes involved events which were puzzling to us. Once, when the leading officer was fast asleep from too much wine, the other officers gave him a false moustache painted on with burnt cork which made him look like Hitler. When he woke up we were scared he might think we'd done it. But the young officers confessed and as a punishment were condemned to cleaning the horses in the stables with the 'Mongols'.

One morning we woke up and my mother said to us: 'The Germans have left.' Even Otto and Clocher had gone. I was unhappy because I had not said goodbye. My mother and Enrichetta called us into our former bedroom. They had opened the windows and drawn back the sheets. The sheets were covered by thousands of coloured moving points. They were fleas and lice. My mother told us that that was what war was about and that bugs made no distinction between Germans, partisans, Fascists or Englishmen. Enrichetta pointed to two cardboard boxes on the desk. They contained Otto and Clocher's previous week's sugar and biscuit rations which they had saved so as to have something to give us on their departure. For years I prayed that the two Germans had got home safe and sound. I wonder if they did?

Isetta and members of her family (bottom).
Tato (top left), Isetta and her grandfather (centre)
and with Tato at her first Communion.

30

A Right Cod of a War

By HUGH LEONARD

Southern Ireland was officially neutral during the war, yet, for the size of its population more men signed up to fight against the Germans than any other country in the world. Hugh Leonard, like every other child waiting for something exciting to happen, managed to develop the knack of missing it when it did.

ATLANTIC

OCEAN

Belfast

IRISH SEA

IRELAND

Dublin • Dun Laoghaire

BRITAIN

ENGLISH

CHANNEL

'There was talk of bombings and poison gas and the end of the world . . .' A gas mask demonstration in Ireland, 1939.

The war was a great disappointment to me. I was twelve when it broke out and, even allowing for the excitement, the news was not allowed to interfere with our Sunday afternoon treat at the Picture House in Dun Laoghaire. For once in my life, however, I paid little attention to the film: I was thinking of how wonderful my life would be once I was evacuated.

There was talk of bombings and poison gas and the end of the world, and I knew that now was my chance to escape from our two-roomed cottage in Kalafat Lane. I would be sent, I believed in my heart, to a great house off in the depths of the country where I would ride horses, become the adopted son of Lord Someone and end up the gentleman I deserved to be.

When we got home from the pictures, I told my mother that bombs would be raining out of the sky at any minute, and she and my father had better look sharp about sending me to safety. Her face went rigid with indignation. 'And do you think we'd desert you?' she said. 'Not at all. You'll stay at home, and we'll all die together.'

I thought it was very high-handed of her. At any rate, it was not the reply I had expected and I had to endure the war at home. Ireland was neutral, of course, and so not only were the next six years for the most part boring, but I seemed to have a genius for missing the occasional good bit.

There was, for example, the night that Dublin was wiped out by German bombs. I was in the sea scouts, and our troop went to spend the weekend camping in a wild and beautiful place of forests and streams about ten miles from where I lived. On the Sunday night, as we huddled around a fire and tried to keep warm, there came rumblings away to the north and we saw flashes in the sky. 'Thunder,' our scoutmaster said. '*I* think,' a scout named Fatboy Brennan (who was actually as thin as a rake) said out of the corner of his mouth, 'it's a German air raid.'

Other people did, too, for early next morning it was my turn to cycle the two miles to Enniskerry village for milk and bread. 'If you please, was there an air raid last night?' If the man behind the counter winked at the woman he was serving, I did not see it. 'An air raid?' he said. 'God help us, sure all the sea coast from Bray to Dublin is wiped out. Gone up in flames. Obliterated.'

Not sparing a thought for the troop's breakfast, I left the milk and bread where they were on the counter, leaped on my bicycle and started to pedal for home. We lived, I should say, half-way between Bray and Dublin: smack in the middle of the area of devastation. As I pedalled furiously, it seemed to me that everyone was going about their normal business. In newspaper photographs of air raid damage in London and such places, I had seen placards saying: 'Britain Can Take It!' It was obvious that Ireland could take it, too.

Along the way, I thought I saw a bombed-out cottage, but it was only falling to bits from age. And I had an acute feeling of disappointment on seeing that our town, Dalkey, was as boringly in one piece as it had always been.

I was not bloodthirsty. I did not want death and destruction. But in a small corner of my mind I longed for change, for anything to break up the boredom. The war, far away across the Irish Sea, was at least eventful and I had personally come to feel that it was thumbing its nose at my friends and me, as if we were not quite good enough for it. Refusing to be passed over, I tried to become a ship's wireless operator, but was told that twelve was not quite old enough, and besides my mother would have killed me.

Next, I joined what was called the Emergency Communications Corps, the idea being that if war came and the telephone system was destroyed, boys on bicycles would carry vital messages. I was not allowed to use my own bicycle, but was given a massive boneshaker together with an armband and a tin helmet. On my first exercise I discovered that freewheeling was impossible – the rear wheel was 'fixed' and the pedals kept turning no matter what. Carrying a message in my pouch, I was speeding down a steep hill towards Dalkey harbour when, forgetting about the fixed wheel, I decided to take a rest from pedalling.

I was at once lifted out of the saddle and deposited, unharmed, in a hedge, from which I could see the bicycle carry on without me down the harbour slipway like a ship being launched. It disappeared beneath the waves, so that now I was accused of losing government property as well as defecting from the sea scouts and stealing their breakfast money.

The war, I told myself, was turning out to be a right cod of an affair, but what proved it was the night I spent in Willie Cunningham's house overlooking the seashore. It was a great thrill to sleep away from home, and I had done so only once, on the painfully remembered scout weekend. As it happened, my own home was less than half a mile from Willie's, but it was nonetheless exciting to go to bed in a box-room high up under the eaves and be lulled to sleep by the soft crash of the waves.

That was a momentous moment in our town's history, for a drifting mine was washed ashore in the small hours and exploded. Great damage was done; roofs were torn off and windows broken. Mrs Cunningham woke up screaming, snatched her seven children from their beds and, still imitating an air raid siren, flung them one by one into the front garden where they all lay face down on the gravel waiting for the next German bomb to fall.

The entire town had been awakened by the explosion, and my parents' first thought was that the

Dalkey – 'as boringly in one piece as it had always been'.

apple of their eye might have had his component parts scattered over a half-mile radius. They put on some clothes and ran down to the Cunninghams' house. Mrs Cunningham had by now stopped screaming, but when my mother asked what had become of me, she started up all over again and at enhanced volume, for she had forgotten about Willie's overnight guest in the box-room.

My father went tearing through the house, accompanied by two men from the fire brigade, which had just arrived. They found me lying peacefully asleep on the floor of the box-room, where I had been blown by the explosion. I had not even woken up. The bed itself was littered with broken glass. When, to loud cheers from the onlookers, I was led out of the house yawning and rubbing my eyes, one would think that my mother and Mrs Cunningham were in a race as to who would faint first.

Next day, as I saw the front page headlines and heard the gossip on every street corner, I knew that I could sink no lower. My dream had come true; the war had at long last visited our town and I, to my everlasting shame, had slept through it.

33

The Burning of Rotterdam

By JOANNA KLOOTS

In the spring of 1940 Hitler declared war on the Dutch. On 10 May the German troops entered like thieves in the night and invaded the country. Joanna Kloots was seven when her world in the city of Rotterdam was turned upside down.

NORTH SEA

HOLLAND

• Amsterdam

Rotterdam

BELGIUM

GERMANY

Joanna lived in the large white building by these bridges, overlooking the river Maas. It was a perfect location for the Germans to watch over Rotterdam.

I was an only child. I lived in a bank where my parents were housekeepers who looked after the people who worked in the building during the day. My father was in charge of general things like keys and the post. My mother took care of the canteen. She made coffee and lunch for the office workers. Our apartment was on the top floor of the building right under the roof, and it had a large balcony. I remember that balcony very well. I played there often and I had a magnificent view over the river Maas and two bridges – the railway bridge and the 'Williamsbridge'. There were only office buildings and hotels in that part of Rotterdam so there weren't many children in the neighbourhood to play with.

I didn't mind this at all because I had a huge and exciting building to play in and everybody treated me very kindly. They taught me typewriting and let me play with the telephone switchboard! Then came 10 May. It was very early morning, and I was asleep but woke up because of noises I had never heard before like distant explosions, the roar of engines and gunfire. My father was standing on the balcony outside the living room and shouted: 'My God, this is war!'

A makeshift bomb shelter in Rotterdam.

Jews being sent away to concentration camps became an all too familiar sight in Holland.

The burning of Rotterdam, May 1940.

The two bridges right in front of the bank were the reason the war came to our doorstep. Hundreds of German soldiers came down by parachute, waterplanes landed on the river and commandos climbed the bridges and invaded the city. My father said: 'Let's go to the cellar and hide there. That's safer. We see what happens tomorrow.' We dressed but forgot to put on our shoes. We hurried down (in our slippers) to the basement where several cellars had been built some years before. I remember I took a doll with me. And our little dog Teddy of course. In the cellar were campbeds and blankets. No food. No water. I was very frightened. We stayed in the cellar all day and my father went back up once or twice to get something to eat and drink. Then suddenly, in the early evening I think, I heard voices the other side of the door, German soldiers! My father had to open the door and I daren't imagine what would have happened if we had been Jews.

From that moment on the Germans occupied the building. We were taken prisoner for five long days and nights. We were probably some of the first people in Holland to be imprisoned by the Germans. But I must say that these 'new inhabitants' were very kind to me. They offered me chocolate and played with me. I remember one soldier who could draw very well. My parents asked the Germans to let us go. They didn't, for fear of betrayal. My father was allowed to go upstairs and he came back with some personal things like toothbrushes and photo albums. The building was already very damaged by that time, as the fight for the bridges was intense. Wounded soldiers were brought in and my father had to help dress wounds.

Despite putting complete trust in my parents, I was afraid and cried because of the gunfire that went on night and day. During the night my mother put cotton wool in my ears. The soldiers brought us something to eat every day, usually black bread and ham which they stole from other Dutch people, no doubt.

On the fourth day the German officer in charge of our bank ordered us and his soldiers to move to another part of the cellar where it was thought to be safer. At two o'clock that afternoon German Heinkel planes bombarded the city of Rotterdam for ten minutes. 24 000 houses were destroyed, 900 civilians were killed and there I was, sitting in between my parents in a safe cellar surrounded by enemy soldiers who sang songs to blot out the terrifying sounds of the bombs for a little fair-haired Dutch girl. This is the way I remember the bombing of Rotterdam.

The next morning we were allowed to go. Holland had surrendered. When we walked out of the bank there were dead bodies in the street and I saw that the city was burning. But we had each other and, with Teddy, we went to an aunt of mine who lived nearby. All our belongings were destroyed and I never saw my house again. Five dreadful years later I was twelve and the war had come to an end.

Joanna, aged seven, with her beloved dog Teddy.

War in a Wheelbarrow

By TOWYN MASON

Not much happened in New Hedges, a sleepy Welsh hamlet nestled in the agricultural heartland of South Wales. Even the menfolk didn't don uniforms and fight at the front. Their agricultural skills were too vital to Britain's survival to be spared. But the war did bring its moments – and its evacuees – as Towyn Mason, the village blacksmith's son, describes.

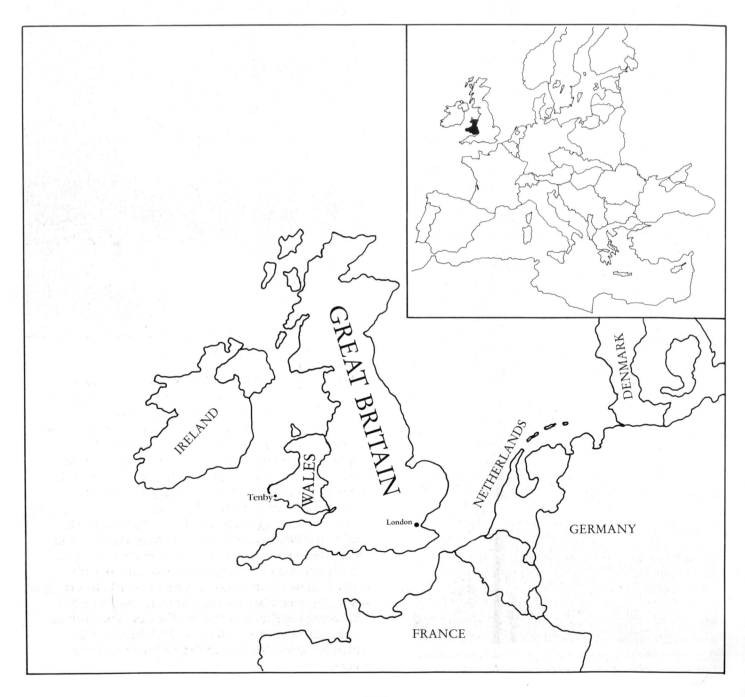

Have you ever slept out of doors in a wheelbarrow? Probably not. But when I was a small boy that was how I sometimes spent part of the night! It was August 1940, about a year after the war between Germany and Britain had begun. I was five and I lived with my father, mother, elder brother, a dog, a cat or two, a canary, several chickens and, from time to time, a pig, in New Hedges, a hamlet not far from the seaside town of Tenby in South Wales.

My father was the village blacksmith, whose job was to mend farm equipment and shoe the horses that in those days did the jobs that tractors do today. Unlike most men he was not 'called up' to join the fighting forces but was allowed to carry on with his work. This was because he helped farmers in their important job of growing food for the cities. I was luckier than many children, whose fathers had to go away to fight, and sometimes never returned.

Everybody knew a terrible war raged in Europe – it was reported daily in the newspapers and on the wireless, and even we had to take some precautions. For instance, at the village primary school we all had to practise putting on gas masks to protect us if poison gas bombs were dropped. The gas mask was made of rubber and fitted tightly over your head and face so that no gas could get inside. There were two eye-holes covered with transparent celluloid for you

to see out, and in front was a sort of round muzzle which you breathed through and which contained some chemical to stop the gas having an effect. When you had your gas mask on you looked like a cross between a rubber pig and a man from outer space, and your voice sounded distant and muffled. Fortunately, there was never any need to use them.

German Air Force map of Pembroke Dock.

For a long time the war had little effect on us – until August 1940. That was when Germany began its big bombing campaign, the Blitz. The raids were mainly aimed at big towns and cities because that was where the factories, ports, railway depots and important buildings which the Germans wanted to destroy were situated. There were no such targets in the middle of the countryside where we lived, but there were several not very far away.

One of these was a place called Pembroke Dock, about 10 miles away, where ships were repaired and where there were big tanks of fuel oil for them. One day a bomb found its target in one of the huge oil tanks. It blew up and caused such an enormous fire that I can remember looking over the garden hedge and seeing the flames in the far distance. The burning oil also created a huge cloud of thick black smoke, which remained hanging in the air for about three weeks.

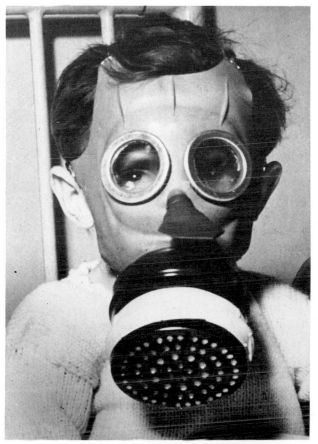

'When you had your gas mask on you looked like a cross between a rubber pig and a man from outer space . . .'

This is how the wheelbarrow comes into my story. As soon as my parents heard the air raid warning - a loud siren that was sounded when it was known that enemy planes were approaching - they would pick me up out of my bed, wrap me in a blanket and pop me, usually still sleeping, into the wheelbarrow outside the back door, while they and my brother sat huddled nearby. As soon as the raid was over and the German planes had gone home I was put back into bed again.

Bomb damage in Tenby.

No bombs ever fell near us, though one did fall in Tenby killing a woman and damaging a few houses. People thought it was probably not intended for Tenby. Most likely, they said, it came from a plane on its way home which found it had a bomb left over after a raid and decided to get rid of it. Also, a few incendiaries - bombs designed to cause fires - were dropped on farms, but the only damage they did was to set a hayrick or two alight.

One evening, in the autumn of 1940, an evacuated woman from London and her two sons walked through our front gate, introduced themselves and moved in. The sons were about the same ages as my brother and myself, and at first we were excited to have them living in our house. But I'm afraid we didn't get on very well with each other. Although London was only about 250 miles away, the evacuees were almost like foreigners to us. I expect we seemed the same to them. In those days most people could not afford to travel very far from home, and none of my family had been to London. The evacuees had never been anywhere else. As a result, we did not know much about each other's way of life. For instance, I had never heard of baked beans until one day the woman opened a tin she had bought and gave me some to try. I thought they were the most

delicious food I had ever tasted. They lived off tinned food much of the time, but we had hardly seen it. On the other hand, they were surprised to see chickens wandering about in the garden and cows grazing in the fields around us.

So both families were a bit suspicious of each other. The evacuees thought New Hedges a very dull place and probably regarded us as primitive peasants. In fact, they certainly did hold some very uncomplimentary opinions about Wales and the Welsh. For our part, we considered the evacuees rude and rough. We thought it very strange that the younger boy used to go to bed with his boots on and that they all slept downstairs in the same room, even though there was a bedroom upstairs which the boys could have used.

The evacuees stayed with us for about eight months and then decided to go home. I think they found life in New Hedges so boring that they preferred to be back in London, despite the danger. But it showed us how lucky we were that we were not forced by bombing to leave our home and go to live in an unfamiliar place. Other evacuees, however, enjoyed being in a different part of the country, and some liked it so much that they never went home, even after the war was over.

A government poster urging mothers not to return their children to the cities.

The Morgan family from Tenby and their 'family' of evacuees.

As a child I naturally did not understand much about the war. In fact, I thought the whole subject very boring, except when children's competitions were held to do paintings of RAF planes. But I could not keep it out of my head altogether. For example, at one time I pretended I had a secret friend called 'Leel' who played with me in the garden. Where did the name Leel come from? Probably from the wireless, when it reported that the French town of Lille (pronounced Leel) had been captured by the German army.

But my brother was very interested in the war and liked to play games with me about it. One of these games was to award me medals for deeds of great bravery, as if I was a soldier and he was a general. The most difficult medal to win was the VC - the Victoria Cross - which was kept for the most daring exploits. I won it twice for jumping off a high wall that ran along the side of the garden into the field next door. I also won the DFC (Distinguished Flying Cross) and the DSO (Distinguished Service Order) for other such displays of outstanding courage.

Later in the war, when British planes began bombing raids on Germany, we learnt what real courage was. Early one Sunday morning in February 1943, when we were all in bed, there was a knock at the door. Not knowing who it might be, my father went downstairs, picked up an iron poker in case it was somebody dangerous and opened the door. It was a young airman, whose plane had been hit by anti-aircraft fire while on a bombing mission over the German city of Frankfurt, and who had parachuted to safety on the way back because the plane was going to crash. He had landed just across the road. My father brought him in and we gave him some breakfast while he told us all about the raid he had been on. He also told us that he was twenty-one and that he came from Cumbria. Later, my father took him off to a farm nearby where another member of his crew had landed. The rest of the crew had also been able to parachute out of the plane, though one had fallen into the sea and drowned. Our airman was very upset about the death of his friend. He was also sad because they had taken a canary in a cage with them on the mission for good luck and they had had to leave it behind when abandoning the plane. We realised that the young men who had to go on these bombing raids, night after night, were truly brave, because often their planes were shot down and they were killed.

I have many other memories of the war, such as the time when an American soldier came into my father's workshop. In 1941 the Americans joined the war on our side, and some of them were sent to the Tenby area to practise for the big invasion of France which took place in 1944 and which eventually brought about the defeat of Germany. Like all my friends, I longed to meet an American soldier because we had heard that if you went up to one and said boldly 'Got any gum, chum?' he would immediately produce some chewing gum from his pocket and give it to you. The trouble was that, when I finally saw one standing in front of me, chatting to my father, I was so overcome with shyness that I was unable to say a single word! Fortunately, the soldier guessed what was going through my mind so I got my chewing gum without even asking.

But my strangest memory of the war is of waking up in the middle of the night and finding myself tucked up in our old wooden wheelbarrow in the garden, looking up at the stars.

The Road to Independence

By PREMILA DEVA

India was still part of the British Empire in 1939, so when war broke out India automatically entered the war with Britain. Premila Deva was the eldest child in a leading Indian military family. For much of the war her father was on active service amidst some of the worst fighting. But he did survive, coming home after Independence to become Commander-in-Chief of the Indian Army.

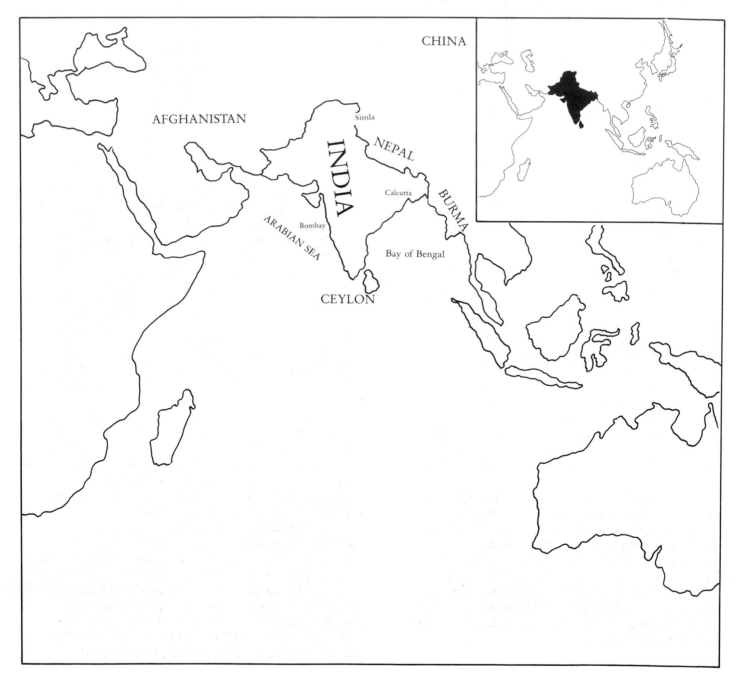

When the Second World War broke out, my parents and I were in Camberley in England where my father was at the Army Staff College. The course was cut short and we returned to India immediately so that he could rejoin his regiment. We sailed home on the 'Stratheden' and travelled by convoy for a short way. After that we were on our own. Somewhere in the Bay of Biscay we encountered a German submarine. It chased us for a bit but we managed to shake it off. However, radio broadcasts reported that the 'Stratheden' was believed to have been sunk. My grandparents in India were terribly worried.

Back in India, life went on fairly normally for me until my father went to Burma in 1941. I remember so well the day he said goodbye. He asked me what I would like him to bring back, and I said I wanted a 'real, live aeroplane'. He was away for a year and for long periods there was no news of him. One day someone told my mother he had been wounded. Naturally no one mentioned this to me, but I remember a gloomy atmosphere at home. During this period, and whenever my father was away, we lived with our grandparents. By now I had a little sister. We were loved and indulged by both grandmothers.

Life in my father's family home was perhaps a little more traditional and disciplined than at my mother's. This grandmother, a devout Hindu, used to have evening prayers in the hall. All the children, the servants and their families were expected to be present. There would be a tremendous amount of hymn-singing, which was great fun.

What I really loved was living in my maternal grandmother's house where there were two uncles to spoil me and a pretty young aunt who let me 'dress up' in her clothes and gave me piano lessons. I remember eating delicious meals in that house. My aunt used to call me 'Appo' because of my huge appetite. So, though there certainly were shortages I don't remember being deprived of anything in the way of food. Sugar, rice and wheat were rationed, so was petrol. White bread was almost impossible to find. But perhaps it helped to be an Army family. Services canteens were well stocked with all sorts of goodies, and I think I ate chocolates right through the war.

While we lived this very privileged life against the backdrop of large bungalows, shady lawns and liveried servants, Bengal was reeling under the worst famine in 150 years. The Government was totally unprepared. Rice imports from Burma had stopped. Petrol was hard to come by and, when Japan entered the war, trains and other forms of transport were taken over by the Government for military purposes. The war had top priority, although millions of people were dying of starvation.

Premila's father was a Subultern before war broke out.

When my father came back from Burma we were in Simla. A few days before he returned I had a very vivid dream. I was sitting near the bay window of the drawing room with a book. When I looked out, I saw him striding down the slope to the house. He waved to me, and as he ran down he fell heavily on his side. Then I saw him in his room with his foot on a stool while his batman unlaced his shoes. He said to me: 'Darling, I couldn't get you the aeroplane but let's go into town tomorrow and buy something else!' Two or three days later this is exactly what happened. I was in the drawing room, he slipped as he ran towards the window, and later in his dressing room he said those very words to me.

During those summer months in Simla I went to a private school run by a Miss O'Brien. One day she said to me: 'Aren't you Indians lucky to have the British to protect you?' I don't remember my reply. Later I repeated this to my father who, just back from a gruelling campaign in Burma, snapped: 'Tell her India is being defended by Indian soldiers.'

Air raid precautions were taken in Bombay and Calcutta. The latter city was bombed a couple of times in the dock areas. I think air raid exercises were held in other sensitive places in order to keep people prepared. I remember seeing bolts of dark blue cloth in a room waiting to be be made up into blackout curtains. I have no recollection, however, of using them. One day in 1942, our *ayah* (nanny) rushed into my mother's room, crying: 'Bibiji, I hear they are going to bomb us!' Great excitement among the children. Nothing happened, though we lived in hope.

There were several camps in India for Italian prisoners of war. These were large barracks or houses in quite unprison-like surroundings. The men generally worked as gardeners or nurses. Some of them were even employed as cooks. They were allowed out with passes and were sometimes invited to tea by the local residents.

When I was six my father went to the Middle East. I can't remember much about his departure, and this time I had no 'visions' about his return! My mother was expecting another child. We divided our time, as before, between our grandparents' homes. I went to another private school belonging to a dear old Englishwoman called Miss Tilt. There were about eight or nine pupils and Miss Tilt had a different kind of cake every day for our elevenses.

Premila (left) with her mother and sister in Simla, 1943.

During this time there were no letters from my father. We knew the war was going successfully. The Battle of Alamein had taken place a year earlier, and Rommel had been routed by the Eighth Army of which the famous 4th Indian Division was a part. Indian soldiers had fought with great gallantry, and many of them, both officers and men, were decorated for their valour.

In 1945 my father came back to India. My youngest sister was eighteen months old. She had never seen him before, and for weeks she absolutely refused to call him anything but 'uncle'. For her 'Daddy' was our grandfather. So, his next campaign was to make friends with his children. He would sit with us and chat. I remember him telling me that he and his

friends would play Bridge in the evenings, and the next morning the winner would get everyone's share of toast. As my father was quite good at the game I imagine he rarely went hungry at breakfast!

Most of my family was connected in one way or another with the Government. My exposure to the world outside this circle was limited, and I was too young to read the newspapers. But even I thought it was odd that while we were fighting to prevent Hitler from occupying other countries, India was occupied by the British. The general feeling though was that a Nazi victory would be disastrous.

In Burma some Indian officers and soldiers had formed the Indian National Army in response to a call from the nationalist leader Subhash Chandra Bose. The aim was to fight the British for independence. This carrot had been dangled in front of our noses for years and many people had become impatient. Opinions were sharply divided about the Indian National Army. They were considered great patriots by many. There were also those who thought they were traitors. It was a great talking point in Army circles.

An overwhelming surge of national feeling was now sweeping over the country. There was a feeling of excitement, not just because the war was over but because Independence was at hand at last. I don't remember the Victory celebrations, but I will never forget the atmosphere of hope for the freedom that had been promised to India for so long.

Closing moments of British rule in India.

The Bomb to End All Wars

By AKIHIRO TAKAHASHI

Defeat ran contrary to everything Japan stood for. In May 1945 their allies, Germany, surrendered. But the Japanese fought on, even when their military situation was hopeless. In August 1945 the Americans dropped two atom bombs: one on Nagasaki, one on Hiroshima. A month later Japan, reeling under the horror of the devastation, surrendered. Akihiro Takahashi was a survivor of the Hiroshima bomb. His experience of that day has led him to devote the rest of his life to the cause of peace.

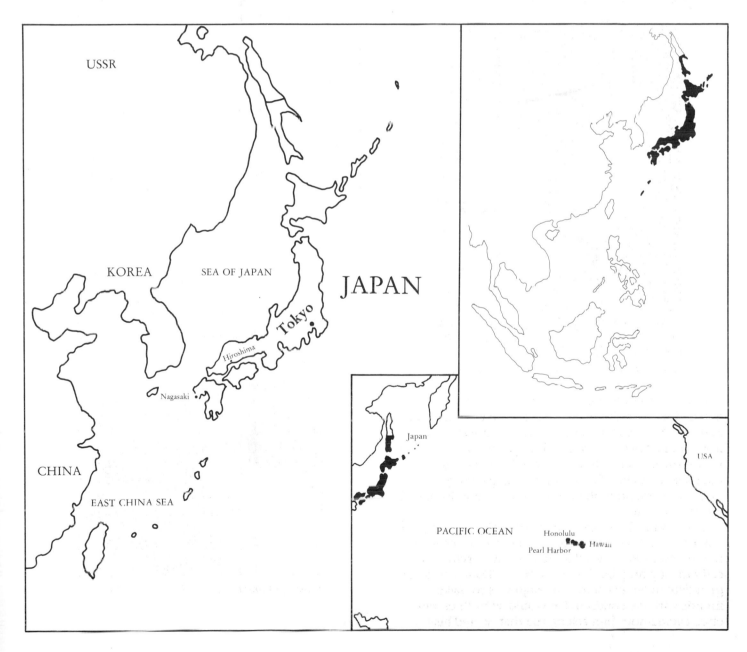

Akihiro (front) with his grandfather and brothers.

August 6 1945. A day I'll never forget as long as I live. Never! That day was to be the last day of my boyhood. The experience I had that day – at the age of fourteen - is too much to bury in the back of my mind, even though the power to forget pain is said to be the strongest among human abilities.

My childhood was that of a typical Japanese boy. My country was dominated by militarism and Hiroshima was a military base. As early as I can remember I wanted to join the navy, like most of my friends in school. The gallant figures of junior pilots of the Naval Air Force fascinated me with their white uniforms trimmed in black braid and buttons, their white caps and short swords. I really wanted to wear a smart uniform like them.

At school, we were taught that the Second World War was a just and holy war for Japan. As part of our school timetable we had military training every day when we vowed that as soldiers we would 'kill as many enemies as possible, to lead our country to victory!'

I turned to kendo fencing and sumo wrestling to grow strong physically. Sumo was a national sport and the Japanese government encouraged it by setting up sumo clubs at schools, shrines and temples. I was often picked to represent my class or school in sumo matches. I particularly remember one episode in a sumo match among elementary schools in Hiroshima City. A boy from my school was in the ring. His loin cloth, which should have been fastened tight, worked its way loose and fell off. He was completely naked. There were cheers and laughter from the boys and screams from the girls. The boy ran to the dressing room hiding his embarrassment with both hands. The match was replayed after he tightened his belt. This vivid scene amid the horror of war still brings a smile to my face.

I remember the sky was clear and blue on 'That Day'. An ordinary, military-minded boy of fourteen, I was just a student of an ordinary secondary school in Hiroshima. Students of my age were sent by order of the government to factories to assist the war effort, to help with emergency drill or to help out on farms.

'That Day', though, happened to be a normal school day and about 150 students, including 60 of my classmates, were just starting the day. The morning began with an outdoor assembly. The schoolyard where we gathered was only one and a half kilometres from the point where the atom bomb dropped. Our class leader was ordering us into line when the sky went pitch black and a shattering noise 'KABOOM BOOM!!' split our eardrums. The next moment there was brown smoke hanging over us. 'What was happening?' I was confused. Five minutes passed, maybe ten. When the pall of smoke lifted, things became dimly visible and I found myself lying about ten metres back from where I had stood. My friends were scattered all over the yard where they had been blown. The school building had totally collapsed, and not a house was standing anywhere in the neighbourhood. They had all been destroyed so far as I could see. 'Hiroshima perished!?' We had no warning that such a thing could happen.

I looked at my own body. My uniform was blasted to shreds. The skin at the back of my head, my back, both hands and both legs had peeled off and was hanging down like rags. My burns were especially severe on both hands and legs, and raw flesh was exposed. Suddenly I was gripped with terror. Yet, confused as I was, the lessons taught over and over again in those daily military exercises came to my aid, maybe saved my life. *'In an air raid,'* this little voice reminded me, *'make for a river!'*

I made my way as best I could towards the river, surrounded by scenes from hell: a man whose flesh was raw from the waist up, a man from whose body jutted broken bits of glass, a woman dripping blood and with one eye hanging from its socket - they were all escaping my way. On the ground I saw a woman dead from stomach wounds, a mother and child red raw, a bloody horse with its head in a watertrough . . . No words or phrases could properly describe this tragedy.

Hiroshima in the aftermath of the atomic bomb. Over half the population died as a result of the fall-out

The deadly 'mushroom' cloud appeared after the bomb exploded.

Every path to the river was blocked by the rubble of shattered houses. I used all my strength to crawl and finally reached the river bank. At that very moment the rubble of houses exploded and long jets of flame shot up in the sky. The whole neighbourhood became one flaming mass. I escaped the new explosion by a hair's breadth.

Among the ruins a small wooden bridge somehow remained intact and I was able to cross it and reach the other side. 'Oh, I'm safe.' With the sudden relief of tension, tears streamed from my eyes. Feeling my body burning I entered the river. The cool water soothed me and seemed more precious than anything else.

I crawled out of the river and made my way to a first aid station that had been hastily constructed in a bamboo thicket. It was about an hour since the bomb fell. There I rested after treatment. Then came the rain. Large, black drops began to fall from the sky. For the first time in my life I saw black rain. 'Is there such a thing as black rain in this world?' I wondered. Then it stopped and I began to walk towards my house. It was about six kilometres from the bomb centre.

On the way I saw my great-uncle and aunt who were returning home from a Buddhist service nearby in the countryside. He did not recognise me and my aunt was very upset to see me but gave me two huge riceballs she had with her for use in an emergency. I ate them straight away. They were so delicious I can remember the taste even now. Our staple diet consisted of bran dumplings, wheat porridge, sweet potatoes and ordinary potatoes and I never had a chance to eat white rice.

With the help of my uncle and aunt I finally reached home. For the next eighteen months every day was spent receiving treatment for my burns. Although close to death several times I survived, thanks to my doctor and the good care of my mother and grandparents.

Atomic radiation caused me inflammation of the liver, and I still need three injections a week to keep me alive. My right hand and arm are permanently distorted and paralysed. The scars of the burns still show on my hands and the nail of my right forefinger still grows black, because a broken piece of glass stuck in it and destroyed the surrounding cells. In the four and a half decades that have passed by since the bomb dropped, I've managed to sustain my health under faltering conditions.

Teenage Japanese fighter pilots in training.

atrocities of war to pass on the unspoken message of the dead to future generations.

This is my message to the children of today. War is nothing but death. War leads to our own death, the death of our loved ones, the death of those we cherish and respect. Terrible atrocities are committed to the innocent and the helpless in the name of the Fatherland. Japan is as guilty as any country of such actions – actions which I deeply regret today.

In nuclear war everybody loses, for atomic warfare results in the destruction of the earth as well as the end of mankind. I know my story is just one of many millions of tragic stories that have been told about the Second World War. I was lucky. At least I survived. There are many millions of people whose story you will never hear. Perhaps by recounting my experience of 'That Day' in 1945 it will help you understand the full horrors of war and of nuclear war in particular.

It may not happen in my lifetime but maybe the children of today, who will be the rulers of tomorrow, will make the stand that we in our ignorance failed to do. Perhaps the next generation will abolish all nuclear weapons and work towards a world of peace and harmony.

A watch records the moment of the tragedy of Hiroshima.

Out of 60 classmates only 11 survived, myself included. About 350 000 people were living in Hiroshima. By 1950 about 200 000 had died as a result of exposure to the atomic bomb. From 'That Day' I pledged to myself that I would devote the rest of my life to the cause of peace. It is the duty of every survivor of the atom bomb, every survivor of the

Only eleven members of Akihiro's class survived the bombing of Hiroshima.

48